Advance the Collective

Book of Quotes and Sayings

AUTHORED AND PUBLISHED BY: ADVANCE THE COLLECTIVE

Copyright © 2024 Advance the Collective

All rights reserved. No part of this book may be reproduced or used in any manner without prior permission from the copyright owner, except for the use of brief quotations in a review.

ISBN: 979-8-9921092-1-4 (paperback)
ISBN: 979-8-9921092-0-7 (ebook)

Published by Advance the Collective

Introduction

The following is a collection of original philosophical and spiritual quotes about life, existence, ethics and perception, slowly and carefully developed through years of meditation, growth, and deep experience. It is an introspective adventure, encouraging pragmatic reflection and inspiration.

Advance the Collective

1. When you've been informed about issues within your responsibility, but you still don't change, you're subconsciously telling the universe that pain is your teacher of choice. Exposure to the truth reveals who is innocent and who won't change.

2. Seek to have your past experience as a full arsenal you can pull from, but without carrying it all the time.

3. Sometimes you must be the drop in the ocean. And sometimes you must be the island in the ocean.

4. Awakening to the truth about society is a burden that is carried for the rest of your life.

5. Take note of which problems in your life are problems that come from issues in your character.

6. There is a difference between caring what people think and letting what they think have a significant impact on your wellbeing. It's fine to care about how others perceive you until it reaches the point where it is harming your ability to be your best.

Advance the Collective

7. The realization of the commonality of insanity is one of the strongest antidotes to gullibility. Question everyone's sanity.

8. In some cases, learning to navigate the brokenness is more important than healing because the unfortunate truth is that you can't heal from the reality of the world around you.

9. Your discipline creates your character.

10. Awareness can often be readily shared, but integrity cannot.

11. The ideal source of happiness is happiness itself. Make it an internal choice every time you can, not reliant on circumstances.

12. Maybe hurt people hurt people, but unhurt, insensitive people can sure do some damage too.

13. Sometimes you can be surprised at how much choice you have in how traumatized you get from something.

14. Sometimes you have to choose between the experience of light and the experience of truth.

15. Remain faithful in the challenge until defeat is fully realized. Try to reserve your tantrum until hope is actually lost.

16. Just because the adversity is stronger sometimes, that doesn't mean your practice and efforts don't work.

17. You can view things as there being three factors that affect how much wellbeing you experience: your naturally-given spirit and abilities, your circumstances, and your will.

18. You are responsible for not remembering where you came from too much or too little.

19. Sometimes you have to create your own light.

20. In this world, morality without strength is death.

21. In life you are left with the decisions you have made and your circumstances. In death, only the former will be what remains.

22. Be cautious of insights that arise in an overload of suffering.

23. It doesn't matter so much who had the greatest effect, but who did their part.

24. No practice will substitute you purposing to be a good person.

25. Being adaptable is good but some things in life are just nonnegotiable and require your stubborn resolve.

26. There are two philosophies to explain the suffering that is experienced: 1. The force of good is weak 2. Your soul previously consented to it.

27. Immaturity and immorality go hand in hand.

28. Good warriors are warriors whether they win or lose. Whether they win or lose, they win spiritually.

29. Witnessing extreme injustice is just a part of life.

30. Nobody said people were going to give you any credit for all the micro decisions that matter the most.

31. Being spiritually asleep is a demon itself.

32. Deep down, either you want to know the actual truth, or you want to think you know the truth and believe what makes you feel good about yourself.

33. As long as you are being diligent in life, there is no reason to feel unfulfilled. It only matters so much if you are seeing results or not, because there will always be hypothetical better results you'd like to see.

34. There is more truth to the dark side people reveal about themselves than the light side, because there is more incentive to fake the light side. So seemingly equal duality observed in someone's character usually implies they are tilted negatively.

35. Embrace that life is an adventure, full of darkness and adversity. Don't look to this life for salvation.

36. False and naive unlimited beliefs can be more limiting than limited beliefs.

37. The best source of security is resilient spirit.

38. Finding stillness in adversity strengthens the spirit.

39. It's not just about one's direct struggles, but their specific level of vulnerability to them.

40. Some things in life require absolutely nothing less than supernatural strength.

41. You don't need money, sex, relationships, good health or even happiness to have spiritual wealth and dignity.

42. You never know what you might have waiting for you.

43. Mystical wellbeing contains the best sensations one can experience.

44. It's easier to master the facade of maturity than it is to master maturity.

45. Strength is usually a choice.

46. There are those who take more pride in their gifts and there are those who take more pride in their choices.

47. Subtle actions can reflect not-so-subtle truths about someone's character.

48. Some shit is just written in the stars.

49. Don't be surprised by someone's poor character.

50. Positive people are not always good people.

51. There is competition in almost everything in this world. Don't compete at something unless you are better than the average person who would take your place.

52. It's not necessarily about what is natural, but about what is harmonious.

53. There are two versions of the experience-the version where you close energetically and the version where you remain open.

54. Perhaps it is the human perspective that strictly values perceived health and happiness, and the cosmic perspective that values growth and expansion. And though the growth and expansion

can include and lead to health and happiness, there is still only so much overlap in these perspectives.

55. Discomfort is a game of tolerance, and on one side you have hesitant and resentful tolerance, and on the other you have embraced and empowering tolerance.

56. Relaxation is a paradoxical discipline, but should often be considered a discipline nonetheless.

57. It's not about doing everything you can to make a certain change.

    It's about taking the right course of action to make the change.

58. The perception of time is an entire system within you that should ideally have an on/off switch that you have access to. You can so simply close the doors to so many negative spirals by just flipping that switch when it is important to do so.

59. Let fear guide and work you into balance, not into submission.

60. Sometimes the real practice is learning to enjoy the practice.

61. Learn as much as you can from others 'mistakes, but realize that it doesn't always serve you best to learn from others 'mistakes when your path plays by different rules.

62. I like to think that any darkness through which I remain in my power is simply added to my power.

63. The real solid foundations actually lie beyond the solidity of the physical world. It is physicality that tends to be more flimsy than the internal and energetic structures that precede it.

64. Become sensitive to the darkness and numb to the fear.

65. Always searching for ultimate truth can distract from your truth.

66. The nature of suffering is apparent meaninglessness and the stripping away of sacredness. It is your job to infuse your suffering with sacredness.

67. Lean toward the side of taking things lightly, but still pay the due respect and awareness to those things. Don't necessarily be quick to take things seriously, but be quick to power up your

consciousness over them, which is a subtle form of taking them seriously.

68. To master an overall balance, you must learn to master counterbalancing on the micro level, which involves experiencing imbalance while maintaining an understanding of the bigger picture. There are those who only view lack of balance as a need for the side that is lacking, and there are those who remember to view it ultimately as an overall need for balance.

69. Things can quickly change for the better once the right changes are activated. A fan can sit unused and collect dust for an indefinite period of time. But once you turn it on, it doesn't matter how much dust there is or how long it has been there. It is blown away.

70. You don't fear so much what could happen with the extensions when you have the strong foundation. And resilience to fear is the strong foundation.

71. Maturity is lame, until you realize it's where the power and strength is at.

72. Sometimes the light is brightest on its edge. There can be a lot of magic on the front lines.

73. There are those who respond to blessings with gratitude and there are those who respond with pride.

74. Perfection requires just as much acceptance as it does effort and adjustment.

75. Don't let your sense of closure and clarity depend on things going as you had consciously or subconsciously expected.

76. Every time you are in your fear, it is yet another battle between a sentient being and fear, but it is unique, new, and how it plays out has yet to unfold.

77. It doesn't matter if you're helping others if you're not doing the right thing.

78. Kindness is no substitute for awareness. It only takes one unkind person to convince innumerable kind people who lack awareness to help fulfill their unkind agendas.

79. You don't have to have a clear mind to have a still mind. You don't have to be so careful of the thoughts you think when you are the observer of them.

80. All you've ever needed is a healthy state of consciousness, even if you have to navigate and/or fulfill a whole slew of somewhat inconvenient and illusory human programs to get there.

81. The question is not "do you believe in A higher power?" It's "do you believe in higher power?"

82. Value access over possession.

83. Natural expression is cool and all, but that doesn't mean you should avoid choosing higher states over negative natural expressions like anger, sadness, stress, etc whenever it's within reach to do so.

84. Make consciousness one of your things.

85. Not suffering is worth suffering for.

86. Flow is not just acting on impulse. Sometimes it is even created through the disruption of unfocused impulse.

87. Sometimes you've got to prioritize happiness itself over what makes you happy.

88. Sometimes ignorance is bliss, but oftentimes it is just the belief system of bliss, and not the actual experience of bliss.

89. Ignorance might be bliss sometimes, but rarely for anybody other than yourself.

90. Don't assume life is trying to teach you something, but always see what you can learn and what it could be teaching you regardless.

91. It's not always about how evolved you are, it's about how good you are at being however evolved you are.

92. It is important to realize when symptoms are not the actual root cause of something, but also avoid tossing symptom

management out the window with that realization, because you never know when the symptoms are a gateway to the root cause.

93. I've got good news and bad news. This isn't over yet.

94. Care about less. Care for more.

95. When you consistently come through on what you tell yourself you are going to do, it creates a pattern in your subconscious and program in your character. That is why it is not only important to have the discipline to follow through on those things, but to have the self-awareness and wisdom to avoid setting out to do things you are not ready for or capable of. When you're always trying to be stronger than you are, you begin to view yourself as weak and become weak because you don't know the sensation of being strong and lifting weight you can actually handle.

96. The energy you experience from someone when you are with them is not just their energy, but also the energy your presence invokes in them. It is just a version of them.

97. If your best isn't good enough, then that's not on you.

98. Go all in in this life, trusting you've got a lot more outside of what you're playing with.

99. Whatever you are going through or experiencing, remember it is just your turn now.

100. Sometimes everything that is blocking up your heart is actually all in your head.

101. When you lose touch with "the devil," you may lose touch with "God" because "God" is not one of denial and ignorance.

102. Don't listen to what the pain and hurt is telling you. Focus on what it could be teaching you.

103. Your life's work extends beyond your occupation.

104. Don't give your power away to proving your power.

105. Things are not black and white. You see, they are and they aren't.

106. Notice how your feelings affect your thoughts and intelligence.

107. What does the socially conditioned mind and an underage drinker have in common? They both go around with fake identifications.

108. The most fundamental thing to put your heart and soul into is your heart and soul.

109. There's the kind of expansion where you come back to your foundation better off and there's the kind where you are there to establish new foundation.

110. One of the best things you can do to help people is overcome your fear of their experience while maintaining some empathy.

111. Invalid confidence usually comes from insecurity.

112. You may gain power by having strength when you don't have any.

113. Sometimes the universe is more of a personal trainer than a teacher and it's not so much about the lessons as it is about the exercise.

114. Sometimes, slow and steady, with the occasional phase of not moving at all, and the occasional phase of moving unsustainably fast, wins the race.

115. "It's always something" when you never make time to abide in nothing.

116. If integrity was always just choosing light over darkness, everyone would have it. Integrity is choosing darkness over the fake light.

117. Neutrality isn't always balance.

118. It's good to keep things simple, but not plain.

119. Sometimes the best novelty is not found in new things, but in the more uncharted territory of committed mastery.

120. Fluoride has been intentionally added to the water supply. When consumed, it concentrates in the pineal gland (Cunningham,

2021). Studies have shown links between fluoride intake and lower intelligence (Gopu, 2022). Drink filtered water such as reverse osmosis water.

121. It's not the people that take your power that end up with it. For some reason it tends to end up in the hands of something unseen and no one actually gets it.

122. Don't try to be the controller when you are the navigator. When you overly control, you clench, but when you navigate, you flow.

123. The issue to be mindful of is that the path to truth and advancement is often based in contrarianism, which tends to be based in ego, resentment, and illusion.

124. It's not about getting off. It's about being off.

125. You take what you can get in life and the rest of the time you just be a strong-ass mother fucker.

126. The secret to adaptability is not really the lack of commitment like it may seem. It is commitment-commitment to what is relevant.

127. Imbalanced action taking place in the state of still observation is like a flame burning underwater. Meditation is pretty much the closest thing to purity.

128. When suffering is transmuted, it can be perhaps the most powerful currency with which the extraordinary is purchased.

129. It is often the case that the people who are where you want to be in the future have been some version of where you are now.

130. You are a creator of your reality.

131. Don't assume that any group or demographic of people are any less likely to be crazy and incorrect than anyone else.

132. Sometimes you can suffer for other people, but you can't learn their lessons for them.

133. Humans are creatures of habit. The question is if you are the version that is a creature of consistency and diligence or the version that is addicted to the comfort zone of unconsciously and stagnantly doing the same thing again and again.

134. It doesn't matter if you're caught with your pants down if you're a nudist.

135. You create to serve yourself and others, or you create to receive empty affirmation from others.

136. If you don't want to play the game, sometimes your best bet is just winning it.

137. It doesn't really matter whether you count on some guru for truth or some mainstream news network. Until you personally take responsibility for shedding your own ignorance, you will be a sheep (no offense).

138. The sooner you accept the challenges you have to, the better. Just be sure to double check to make sure you actually have to.

139. If you can't let go of the old, focus on building the new. If you can't build the new, focus on letting go of the old. If you can't do either, be still for now.

140. It's not necessarily about following your heart, but following your heart when it is in the right place. Following your heart when it is in an imbalanced and volatile state can be a very dangerous course of action.

141. It's not just about surrendering what you can't control. It's about surrendering what you shouldn't control.

142. People can be shown things, but ultimately, we have to see for ourselves.

143. Sometimes you just gotta trust that you will be rewarded for your pain.

144. There are many lives to be lived within this life.

145. Always be prepared to experience temporary failure.

146. You can create love out of darkness, but that's not always a good thing when you create just enough love to keep you stagnantly content with something that requires deeper resolve. We can

scrape the love out of our unsustainable practices until one day we can't anymore.

147. Hard truths delivered aggressively are rarely received well.

148. Avoid being in a state of waiting for anything other than higher consciousness.

149. It's not about being above having a breaking point, because you will always have one. It is about being above your breaking point, and being grateful for it.

150. The least you can do is mean well.

151. It's the stupidest things that cause the most suffering.

152. Live and unlearn.

153. Consciousness is resilient enough to be capable of experiencing heaven after hell.

154. You can view your suffering as your oppressor and identity or as your sacred work and challenge for right now.

155. Security doesn't come so much from your trust in your connection to the light, but your trust that your connection to the light will always return.

156. Humanity is more concerned with creating convenience than with reducing its suffering. We live in a system where the expansion of the latest iphone sales take priority over healthy human living conditions.

157. You are ahead of everyone on your journey.

158. Many people should push themselves more, but remember that always pushing your limits is all fine and well until you realize you are doing it from a place of a form of poverty mindset where you feel like there is never enough, and that psychological programming is your real limitation that needs to be pushed.

159. There's nothing you can do about it just means there's nothing you have to do about it.

160. Emphasis on thinking and emphasis on feeling both have their place. However, thinking tends to confine you to a limited

spectrum of experience. When you focus on feeling, you may expand the potential for experience.

161. Don't let feeling good be a reason to adopt ignorant feel-good beliefs. It is like picking a flower expecting it to continue to grow.

162. Gullibility is one of the strongest foundations for imbalance.

163. There's a difference between being self-centered and being centered in self.

164. Don't just look on the bright side. Give life to it and transmute the situation to the bright side.

165. Though both enable you to tolerate its presence, there is a difference between desensitizing yourself to fear and developing the ability to hold your space in fear.

166. It is common to associate strength with tensity. Instead, relax into your strength.

167. If you have decided that turning back is not an option, then embrace it 100%.

168. Sometimes breakthroughs require energy that has been trapped. Respect the necessary uneventful and boring periods, as it is during these periods that energy builds before it will expand out.

169. Standing your ground isn't all about stubbornly letting everyone know how much you're standing your ground. It takes place within and is often best done silently.

170. The masses tend to be kind of the underbelly of the collective.

171. Practice believing that vast states of peace and completeness can be accessed without external stimuli.

172. Think through whatever you have to think through in order to give yourself permission to be mindful.

173. If you can find peace within you while watching foolish and uncompassionate people be rewarded in life for no reason, it's over. You have pretty much won the matrix.

174. In most cases, if you don't have a plan for your life, then getting a plan for your life should be your current plan. Though it shouldn't be rushed, it is a waste of your power to not have a well thought out, tentative plan for your life.

175. Only consider it acceptable for you to either be experiencing value, creating value, or experiencing completely unavoidable suffering, which still may be valuable.

176. Just because the darkness has used something as a vehicle to harm someone does not mean that what it used is inherently dark. And just because the light has used something as a vehicle to bless someone does not mean that what it used is inherently light.

177. In the state of patience, you can connect with the fulfillment of whatever you are being patient for, making it so that you don't really have to be as patient anymore. The more patient you are, the less patient you have to be.

178. It doesn't matter how many crazy spiritual and esoteric experiences you've had if you still live from the ego and you lack any significant self-awareness.

179. Being a good person pretty much comes down to one thing- stewardship-seeking to use your time, resources, energy, and awareness as efficiently and harmoniously as possible.

180. Love is love whether it comes from within or without. But it is true that when you only seek love outside of yourself, you are vulnerable to not experiencing any at all.

181. Either after having had so little, you will be programmed to always experience lack no matter how much you have, or you will do the subtle reprogramming on yourself so that you are instead especially ripened to deeply appreciate all that you have when you do have more abundance

182. Don't let the pain in your body or emotions sweep your mind into experiencing the perhaps greater pain of irrelevant negative thoughts. Experiencing pain within yourself is not a reason to send your mind off to connect to all the other pain of the world. Sometimes it takes the most strength to just not explore the

unnecessary suffering that is not relevant to you right now, even though its exploration will work you the hardest.

183. When the universe works you out way harder than you normally would, you may as well enjoy the big muscles.

184. It is playing out.

185. Your perceptions of the past, future, and the experience of others come to you through the filter of the experience and feelings that are present with you now.

186. Hear the message. Do the message.

187. Resilience is the only way to get through some of this stuff.

188. Life, and your focus, should pretty much just consist of a coming together and give and take between the cultivation of your wellbeing and the cultivation of what gives you purpose.

189. Even if the universe doesn't come through for you, at least you can honestly say that you did your part, just as long as you do your part.

190. Think of an hour of passionate work as exponentially more productive than an hour of non-passionate work.

191. Before bed every night, briefly reflect on how you spent your day and observe where you poorly used or wasted your time, energy, and overall consciousness, and notice things that you are reasonably capable of doing better next time. Keep a to-do list as well as a "have-done" list to see where your time has gone.

192. The best long-term investment is in the present.

193. Sometimes it's about learning your lesson and sometimes it's about putting in your time.

194. There is almost always someone who has risen from worse.

195. Sometimes integrity is one of those things that simply wanting it is having it.

196. A very common and very primitive mistake that people make is thinking that whatever resonates strongly with them at that time of their life applies to everyone.

197. Sometimes when you stop bringing unnecessary suffering upon yourself (such as bad habits), deeper layers of suffering that is necessary are brought up. It can be the fear of those deeper layers that causes one to continue to sabotage themselves with unnecessary suffering.

198. Understand your weaknesses. Know thy shitty self.

199. Mindfulness meditation, reflection, and careful research are three fundamental human practices that most people probably don't make enough time for.

200. It's not necessarily that you shouldn't try to change people, but that you shouldn't try to change people that you can't, and to think more in terms of generally impacting them beneficially.

201. You can think of meditation as a compression of the value spectrum in which you may normally perceive thoughts. It is like seeing the thoughts of varying importance as simply thoughts and therefore seeing them all as somewhat equally important, or equally unimportant as the case may be.

Advance the Collective

202. Balance needs room to breathe and flow. As a result, it can be difficult to try and control balance. It is usually best to "control" it through protecting against excessiveness, as it is usually easier to know what is imbalanced than to know what is balanced.

203. The thoughts you've got to be careful with are those ones that make you perceive large periods of time. Remember the thoughts are still only briefly taking place in the present moment.

204. At times, it is best to just remind yourself that the good stuff is out there, and let the extent of your philosophical thoughts end there.

205. The sense of accomplishment that you should be most concerned with experiencing is the sense of accomplishment in knowing you are doing your best.

206. There is a time to be more heavily goal-oriented and there is a time to be more heavily immediate freedom-oriented. It's important to recognize those times for what they are as well as possible.

207. When they say "it's a marathon, not a sprint," it implies that there is a given distance that must be covered either way-a given amount of energy that must be invested. But with some things, it has less to do with the distance or energy that must be invested into something for it to come to fruition, and more to do with time. Some things require a certain amount of time, and cannot be expedited no matter how much energy is invested into them in the meantime.

208. Money should be some of your power, not have all of your power.

209. When a muscle is broken down, it is only a question of if it receives the proper care and nourishment to rebuild even stronger or if it remains broken down. And this can be metaphorical for other aspects of yourself.

210. The receiving of information from others should first and foremost be an exercise of your own discernment.

211. Sometimes you just gotta hold faith, and just let yourself bathe in your suffering.

212. It is difficult to let go of the past when you believe that you are only one version of you.

213. Help to justify the inherent negativity of your footprint through cultivating the uniqueness of your value.

214. Strive to be more positive than you are happy.

215. If anything should matter to you, it should simply be your experience of reality and your influence on reality.

216. Both too high of standards/expectations and too low of standards/expectations are forms of a poverty mindset. When your standards are too low, you accept poverty and unnecessary suffering. And when your standards are too high, things will never be enough, which is poverty as well.

217. Sometimes the point of empathy isn't about knowing what it's like to be someone else, but knowing that you don't know what it's like to be someone else.

218. The more you can trust yourself to do your best without the drive of desire, the more you can allow yourself to be free from living in desire because there is less use for it.

219. If life is going to be hard either way, you may as well experience the hard stuff that might pay off instead of the hard stuff that will make things worse. The pain of strength is better than the pain of destruction.

220. Part of doing your part is doing everything you can to stay in your power amidst others not doing their part.

221. The experience caused by your experience on this earth will likely be of a much greater proportion to that of your experience alone. Your impact can compound to affect multiple beings at once and lasts after you die. But <u>your</u> experience is singular and more temporary.

222. Lack of clarity is not resolved with dogma and forced beliefs that come from fear.

223. It's not about being a workaholic. It's about being a don't-waste-time-aholic.

224. Strength of character is the best substitute for love when love is deficient.

225. When you look at the sources of your suffering, take into account that you can add the words "perception of" before each of them and the result will still be a relatively accurate description of the source of suffering.

226. Most people don't really struggle to work hard, but they struggle to work hard at something they aren't told to do by someone else.

227. If you can't trust your flow, you can't trust your plan.

228. You have the most control over what is most important-your character.

229. With great uniqueness comes great responsibility.

230. It's not about enlightenment. It's about the divine moments.

231. The more important question isn't really if what you wish for will make you happy, but if living without it for now really has to make you unhappy.

232. As a human, external things will have an impact on your quality of life. But that doesn't mean finding moments of completeness within you shouldn't be a top priority.

233. All you really have to do is face reality.

234. It all pretty much comes down to decision making, so make time to reflect and meditate.

235. Everything happens for a reason. And perhaps some things happen for the reason that evil forces are trying to fuck shit up.

236. In the perception of competition, everybody loses to someone.

237. The most important wave of negative energy to avoid reciprocating is the first one.

238. If you uphold strong integrity and awareness, you will be an island.

239. The biggest internal causes of suffering in the world are probably the lack of integrity and the lack of intelligence and awareness.

240. Intelligence is expanded through mindful, careful research and reflection.

241. Maybe it's time we practice a little more old-fashioned hatred of evil.

242. Good holistic health and wellbeing is home.

243. You need the awareness of how the imbalance is overextension and the patience for it to correct. In your patience you remain in power. When you frantically chase the imbalance, you lose your power.

244. If I had to choose, I'd generally rather choose anger for my dark side than ignorance and stupidity.

245. Seek to create independent moments in which you are completely detached from the things of this world.

246. It can be confusing because the non-nutcases and the nutcases preach a lot of the same shit.

247. It's not about choosing higher consciousness instead of everything else. It's about choosing higher consciousness over everything else.

248. After you have explored, it's about finding sustainability.

249. Forget the whole infinite abundance thing. Reasonable limitations teach you stewardship, efficiency, and wisdom. They cultivate and tune your creation skills and they're a lot of what life is about.

250. Think of the biggest thing you waste time doing and prioritize significantly reducing it or eliminating it from your life.

251. Identifying your life's work and dedications should be a top priority.

252. People need to seriously start prioritizing thinking for themselves. Ask yourself where your beliefs came from. Did they

come from your parents, friends, celebrities, politicians, influencers, personal experience, or logical reasoning? Are they there to make you feel as a part of a community, but aren't based in thorough reflection?

253. There are infinite ways to fuck things up, but rarely more than a few ways to get them right.

254. Light and dark may be in each person, but that doesn't mean the proportions are 50/50.

255. There is always someone out there rooting for you.

256. If you're not going to worry about something later, ask yourself how important it is that you worry about it now.

257. It's not just that people struggle navigating the darkness when they're predominantly in it, but they also struggle with consciously directing the light when they're predominantly in it.

258. Working with heaviness doesn't always have to mean having a bad day.

259. Letting go can be the healthy version of giving up. They are related to some extent.

260. There is light and dark, and most everything else is hearsay and speculation.

261. Weird being in style is not justification for chaos.

262. To live well, you must learn to accept those who mean well and execute horribly.

263. You can get all caught up in the confusion of all the different ways it could play out, but at the end of the day, it will only play out one way. In the end it will be simple. There is only what ends up happening.

264. Challenges are only as difficult as how minimal your perception is of a redeeming experience to follow.

265. When the right decision is easy, don't be the person who doesn't make it because it's so easy you can just make it later. Be humble enough to do the easy things now, not falling for thinking they always will be. Be the kind of person that always makes the right decision when the desire is only 50/50 to make the wrong one.

266. There is perhaps no greater detriment to society than to live well enough, while still in the lower ego. It is to use the unparalleled power of wellness for evil.

267. Within is the final destination of the experience, whether it comes from within or externally.

268. Your faith should cultivate your strength, not give it away to ignorance and denial.

269. There is not awakened vs. not awakened. There is only more of your awakening.

270. There's conscious "I don't give a fuck" and there's little bitch "I don't give a fuck."

271. Let your self-imposed limitations be strict enough to keep your life simple and focused without letting them hinder the flow of your potential.

272. Don't seek power, seek *your* power.

273. The energy that comes on the strongest often leaves the quickest. Stay centered.

274. Think of observing negativity as purging it, and identifying with it as acquiring it.

275. If you are unrelaxed, it should be because the energy you are dealing with is unrelaxed, not because you yourself are not relaxing.

276. Life rarely favors your good intentions, and they require your active responsibility to bring them to life.

277. Learn to balance the necessary expression of your negative emotions while recognizing when it is time to just shut them down, stop feeding them, and begin your focus of attention to better experience. Don't confuse processing negative emotions with feeding them.

278. The loser who quickly accepts and moves on from defeat is often better off than the winner who is swept away with victory.

279. Don't waste the valuable pauses in the storm by using them just to dwell on how bad the storm is.

280. Don't trust anyone or anything to do anything. Just trust.

281. Sometimes "all you have to do is breathe," and sometimes, "you have to just breathe!"

282. Negative energy will either snowball and grow or it will reach a hero who transmutes it. It tends to be all or nothing.

283. To be mindful is to take responsibility.

284. Focus on the positives. Notice the negatives.

285. Don't be a slave to your perceptions of what freedom is.

286. There is always an abundance of lack to be perceived if you allow yourself to perceive it.

287. It's not about living your best life. It's about living the best version of this life.

288. If the mental block isn't big enough to stop you, why let it stifle you at all?

289. For darkness to be a good teacher, you must be an especially good student.

290. You never know when you're just gonna wake up one day and things will be better.

291. People who achieve great things sometimes have a healthy dose of masochism. They are capable of finding enjoyment in suffering that may serve a greater purpose. Discomfort doesn't always have to mean displeasure.

292. Strive to be in a constant state of fully being able to handle and tolerate the present moment.

293. Sometimes there is no wave to ride until after you start riding it.

294. Sometimes the solution to pessimism is not to force optimism, but to have awareness of your blindness to the bigger picture.

295. Be cautious expanding your consciousness without also expanding your inner strength.

296. There is rarely a better alternative to navigating stress and challenges than mindfulness. Mindfulness is the fundamental discipline.

297. Not only is feeling like you have to prove yourself to people unhealthy, but the kinds of people who make you feel that way are the kinds of people who won't understand your worth regardless.

298. Assume "whatever it takes" state of mind-not from a place of uncentered desperation, but from a place of devotion.

299. Too many spiritual people will believe anything that's mumbo jumbo.

300. Your practices and lifestyle will only go so far when there is a lesson you are failing to learn.

301. Pretending you're not a victim when you are is gaslighting yourself and tends to come from the prevalent realm of toxic positivity. It should be about being a strong and mature victim, taking responsibility for what you should, and also having

awareness that you aren't the only one going through difficult stuff.

302. Sometimes people do stupid shit because they literally just don't know any better.

303. Your sense of purpose in life is what gives you strength in hardship. Shallow people with shallow, self-centered purposes will have less endurance.

304. Observe before you label. And don't label what you don't understand.

305. The only being you should compare yourself to is the best version of yourself.

306. When you feel stuck, trust in your vastness.

307. Part of life is getting traumatized and having to move forward.

308. When you refuse to look at something just one way or the other, you insist on seeing it for what it is.

309. Don't try to get poured from empty cups.

310. All you know is based on your limited perception of yours and others' experience.

311. Don't just focus on what you can offer, but on what you can offer that others can't.

312. Contentment is about being content with where you are now in relation to your journey and the process, not necessarily about being content with being where you are now permanently or even longer than the short term.

313. There's a difference between trying to control things and influencing things positively to the best of your ability.

314. You experience a certain sense of power when you succeed. You will probably even experience it when you simply make progress. But until then, the means of experiencing that sense of power is to take healthy pride in your diligence.

315. Just because you don't fit in doesn't mean you don't belong.

316. Life is all about finding the island of resonance in the ocean of dissonance.

317. The cost of uniqueness is some form of loneliness.

318. Your life will completely change when you make being decluttered a top priority. Declutter your clothes, declutter your possessions, declutter your social life, declutter your diet, declutter your music playlists, declutter your refrigerator, declutter your expenses and investments, declutter your creations. You will always be wearing your favorite clothes, listening to the best music, and more or less just experiencing and creating the best things you can in life.

319. If you break, make sure that it took an absolutely unfathomable force to make you do so.

320. Sometimes it is best to view life as a challenge.

321. The main value of goals is clarity on priorities and devotion, not so much reaching a certain number or even achieving them sometimes.

322. The numbing of society has resulted in it forgetting the importance of good and the severity of the evil.

323. Suffering almost always comes in the forgetting that there is more to life and existence.

324. When negative energy is triggered within you, your main focus should be on dealing with that negative energy. Don't think about how unfair or messed up the trigger is when there's nothing you can do about it right now. It has already been pulled, and dwelling on it only pulls it again and again, making it release more negative energy within you when you never even dealt with the initial negative energy.

325. Just because it seems like it is never done doesn't mean it has to never be enough.

326. When you focus on what's going right, you focus on your foundation to build from.

327. Don't be the optimistic fool who is blind to the darkness and who judges pessimists being realistic. Be the optimist who consciously chooses optimism because it may be the best course of action and you are capable of it.

328. It is important to be open to the potential beneficial purpose behind anything without ignorantly assuming it.

329. Strength comes in waves. Just because you are not strong enough now doesn't be you won't be soon. Sometimes it is about having just the strength to patiently wait for your strength.

330. It's not that you don't have any control, but that control is a privilege and there are infinite hypothetical ways you couldn't control in which you could lose it all. So it's good to have some humility. You are one careless driver away from losing it all.

331. Connecting to your power in the midst of struggle can be challenging enough as it is without you adding an incorrect belief that something other than connecting to your power is the ideal solution for it at the moment.

332. You just need enough of a particular energy or thing that you can receive or build more of it. That is the turning point.

333. Stubbornness tends to come from the lower ego. Being relentlessly centered is the healthy alternative.

334. In this reality, information-based awareness without power/character-based awareness will only make your life more difficult.

335. Write in a journal at least once a month. Reflect and observe what you're doing and where you are at in life. It provides guidance and clarity in life.

336. It can be hard not to grasp onto distracting things to make you feel better when you are down, but we often grasp onto these things to feel even better when we already are just fine. If you are just okay, then let that be enough. Just be with the neutrality without always having to artificially enhance it.

337. You're only likely to get so far without a reason for fighting.

338. Be grateful for the island of that which takes care of you in the ocean of that which does not.

339. People are mostly programs. The question is if you/higher consciousness were the main ones who programmed you or not.

340. Don't rely on the value of your personality as your sole means to improve the world. Have some focus for what you create.

341. Narcissism should not be admired as confidence.

342. Think of what you want to be remembered for.

343. It is you and your strength, and you and your lack of strength.

344. There will be people who live to do harm, and then make you out to be the bad guy for being angry.

345. Just because you have absolutely every right to be angry and complain does not mean it is always the best course of action.

346. Everything is going to be okay-in this life or the next.

347. Don't let the sharing of your love become the compromise of your power.

348. Realize that a lot of those feelings are just flawed patterning from the past. They are not based on the current reality. They are bullshit.

349. When you are discouraged because you feel like you have struggled with something for a long time, you are often forgetting that the struggle has actually been on and off for that time. It is that realization that allows you to consciously give life and awareness to the periods in between that suffering and let them grow.

350. Sometimes the real battle is in learning to stop taking on the low-level battles you should be above.

351. The more intense the experience, the more powerful its amnesic effects tend to be. Your current reality is all a matter of what's fresh in your memory.

352. Don't let the details impair your focus.

353. It's not always the ones who work the hardest who create the best work. And no, it's not the ones who work the smartest. It's usually the ones who are the most authentic.

354. It's not free will if it costs a shit load of energy, pain, and discomfort. But it's okay if you can still afford it.

355. There is being adaptable and there is quitting every time things get challenging. There can be times when the path of least resistance is the path where you push straight through the resistance without letting it hold you back forever.

356. A lot of the time, you are just being delusional when you think you want anything specific other than a pleasant feeling within yourself.

357. Get off on your ability to not get off from the ego's vanity highs.

358. There's the kind of taking shit seriously where you give away your power to it and there's the kind where you protect your power from it.

359. There tends to be more security in consistently being able to trust yourself to take the next step than in having the entire path laid out before you when the future is uncertain.

360. Open into, but beyond the negative energy in your way. Follow through.

361. It's time to get in on the unseen scene.

362. A rising tide lifts all boats. And the tide raisers have their work cut out for them.

363. The less dependent you are on someone's higher self, the less fear and more understanding you have of their dark side.

364. Sometimes you've got to let your mind just completely check out in order to check in to what is actually going on.

365. Sometimes the game is won by those who are the least hesitant to start over when it becomes clear they have to. Sometimes resilience is having the patience to take a step back.

Advance the Collective

366. Your individuality can be your strength in the midst of suffering. When you lose awareness of it and perceive your suffering as a meaningless drop in the ocean of the abyss of suffering, your self-care, sense of worthiness, and perceived value of your individual experience is compromised.

367. You don't have to see things for what they are to still be aware when you aren't seeing things for what they are.

368. Depending on where you live, on average, you can expect more than one out of every 100 people you see to end up killing themselves ("Data Page: Number of suicides," 2024).

369. When all else fails, trust that forward in time is forward.

370. Your power is not just the power you have access to, but it is limited by your power to harness it.

371. To withstand the initial impact of the blow without getting knocked off center can be to dodge the destructive core essence of it entirely.

Advance the Collective

372. As one awakens to harsh truths, they must learn to find the balance between reverting to ignorance, and overfeeding the negativity with their attention.

373. It's not as much about being in control as it is about not being in fear.

374. Consider fear as what you venture into, and wellness as what you come back to.

375. Instead of wondering how much longer the discomfort will last, maybe think more in terms of how many more conscious breaths it will last.

376. Sometimes when you catch yourself judging people, it is not necessarily about questioning the validity of your judgment of them, but asking yourself if there's anything better you could be doing with your time right now.

377. Hitler didn't kill 6 million Jews. Factory farms and big business are not torturing billions of animals and burning down the rainforest. Unconscious order followers are. It is almost always order followers who bring about the acute mass suffering. Always think for yourself.

378. Don't be too valiant searching for meaning in the negativity when the message is just to move on.

379. For whatever it's worth, it's just energy.

380. Sometimes your limiting past is nothing more than a thought.

381. When you stay too long, it is usually the devil who comes knocking on the door of your comfort zone with the eviction notice.

382. In the negative state, what is positive will likely appear negative, and in the positive state, what is negative will likely appear positive. Be mindful of your current bias.

383. Overindulging in the creativity of others can appear to fill your creative void without providing any fulfillment. It can be ideal to abide in the bracket of entertainment characterized by your own creation instead of the creations of others.

384. It is usually more evolved to think in terms of using finances to advance your work than in terms of using work to advance your finances.

385. It doesn't matter that much what is to blame for problems that are yours now.

386. Logically speaking and based on factual data, the two biggest external, physical sources of mostly avoidable suffering in the world are animal factory farms, and poverty, caused by unreasonably unequal wealth distribution (greed) and poor people having too many children.

387. Contemplate what needs to happen for your life to improve.

388. You are not just the chooser between the two sides of the spectrum you are faced with, but oftentimes you are also the chooser between picking one side, or reconciling the two sides to create a new side.

389. When you experience an unreasonable egoistic desire, you either choose to experience the stress of attempting to satisfy it or you choose to experience the stress of waiting for it to pass, knowing there will be no sustainable satisfaction for it.

390. Although keeping an open mind and expanding your consciousness can liberate you from dogma, it can also open doors to new avenues of gullibility if you do not consciously keep them closed.

391. Generally, the more points you have to prove someone incorrect, the more futile it is to present them even though they may seem to strengthen your position, because the individual is currently too far gone and dissonant to the truth.

392. Do away with all celebrity or politician worship and any significant level of trust in them. Grow up to realize trusting strangers in this world is for naïve children.

393. The ego will either take pride in the lower self or it will deny its existence entirely.

394. Consistently pursue the relaxed, harmonious way of doing things.

395. Be careful following the lead of someone else, especially someone who wants you to follow their lead.

396. The more you have been through, the less empathy and understanding there will be for you. Although it may help to some extent to feel someone understands you, no one will ever truly understand your pain. Your unique scars and expressions of darkness you have faced are yours to experience. And you and spirit are the only ones to truly know it, and that is the only fully transparent relationship you will ever have.

397. In the abyss of darkness, any crazy shit goes, but from outside the abyss, it is all contained within the abyss.

398. Depending on how you look at it, it is impossible to fear what is in the past. And at the end of the day, it's all in the past.

399. Sweden, Denmark, and Finland rank among the happiest countries in the world (Bloom). They also rank among the countries that tax high income earners most heavily (Young).

400.
- An estimated 111 billion animals are slaughtered each year for animal products and the vast majority are kept in factory farm conditions (Ritchie).
- Studies show that eating a plant-based diet reduces risk of death by 12%, extending average lifespan (Sifferlin). Studies show it reduces risk of the following top leading causes of death.
- A meta-analysis from 2017 found that a vegan diet lowered risk of total cancer by 15% (Dinu et al.).
- A 2019 study, totaling over 300,000 participants, by Harvard scientists discovered that a vegan diet can reduce risk of developing type 2 diabetes by 23% (Roeder).

- Studies show that those who eat a mostly plant-based diet are 32% less likely to die from heart disease (Kim et al.).
- Half of the world's habitable land is being used for agriculture alone (Ritchie). Switching to a plant-based diet would reduce agricultural land use by 75%, which would free up about 38% of Earth's habitable land currently being used and drastically increase Earth's occupancy capacity while the population grows more (growing plant-based food for 111 billion animals takes up more space than growing plant-based food directly for the human population) (Ritchie).
- Chickens are four times larger today than they were in the 1950s (Enviroliteracy Team).
- "Since the 1950s, the Food and Drug Administration (FDA) has approved a number of steroid hormone drugs for use in beef cattle and sheep, including natural estrogen, progesterone, testosterone, and their synthetic versions. These drugs increase the animals' growth rate and the efficiency by which they convert the feed they eat into meat" (U.S. Food and Drug Administration).
- "Approximately nine percent – more than 850 million – of the animals reared for food in the United States each year never make it to the slaughterhouse because they have already died from stress-induced disease or injury" (Duke).

Review and Social Media

Thank you for reading. The quantity and quality of the ratings of this book will play a significant role in determining how many people end up reading it. If you feel others could benefit from these quotes, please leave a review on Amazon to support our purpose. Thank you.

Follow us on Instagram for quotes and sayings: @advancethecollective

Bibliography

1. Cunningham JEA, McCague H, Malin AJ, Flora D, Till C. Fluoride exposure and duration and quality of sleep in a Canadian population-based sample. Environ Health. 2021 Feb 18;20(1):16. doi: 10.1186/s12940-021-00700-7. PMID: 33602214; PMCID: PMC7893939.

2. Gopu BP, Azevedo LB, Duckworth RM, Subramanian MKP, John S, Zohoori FV. The Relationship between Fluoride Exposure and Cognitive Outcomes from Gestation to Adulthood-A Systematic Review. Int J Environ Res Public Health. 2022 Dec 20;20(1):22. doi: 10.3390/ijerph20010022. PMID: 36612346; PMCID: PMC9819484.

3. "Data Page: Number of suicides", part of the following publication: Esteban Ortiz-Ospina and Max Roser (2016) - "Global Health". Data adapted from IHME, Global Burden of Disease. Retrieved from https://ourworldindata.org/grapher/number-suicide-deaths [online resource]

4. Bloom, Laura Begley. "Ranked: The 20 Happiest Countries in the World in 2024." Forbes, Forbes Magazine, 22 Mar. 2024, https://www.forbes.com/sites/laurabegleybloom/2024/03/19/ranked-the-20-happiest-countries-in-the-world-in-2024/

5. Young, Angelo. "25 Countries Where the Rich Are Taxed the Most." 24/7 Wall St., 6 Dec. 2021,

https://247wallst.com/special-report/2021/11/21/25-countries-where-rich-are-taxed-the-most/

6. Hannah Ritchie (2023) - "How many animals are factory-farmed?" Published online at OurWorldinData.org. https://ourworldindata.org/how-many-animals-are-factory-farmed [Online Resource]

7. Sifferlin, Alexandra. "7 Ways Vegetarians Live Longer." Time, Time, 24 Feb. 2014, time.com/9463/7-reasons-vegetarians-live-longer/. https://time.com/9463/7-reasons-vegetarians-live-longer/

8. Dinu, Monica et al. "Vegetarian, vegan diets and multiple health outcomes: A systematic review with meta-analysis of observational studies." Critical reviews in food science and nutrition vol. 57,17 (2017): 3640-3649. doi:10.1080/10408398.2016.1138447

    https://pubmed.ncbi.nlm.nih.gov/26853923/

9. Roeder, Amy. "Plant-Based Diet May Lower Risk of Type 2 Diabetes." Harvard Gazette, 9 Nov. 2023, https://news.harvard.edu/gazette/story/2019/07/plant-based-diet-may-lower-risk-of-type-2-diabetes/

10. Kim, Hyunju, et al. "Plant-based Diets Are Associated with a Lower Risk of Incident Cardiovascular Disease, Cardiovascular Disease Mortality, and All-cause Mortality in a General Population of Middle-aged Adults | Journal of the American Heart Association." Journal of the American Heart Association,

7 Aug. 2019, https://www.ahajournals.org/doi/10.1161/JAHA.119.012865

11. Hannah Ritchie (2021) - "If the world adopted a plant-based diet, we would reduce global agricultural land use from 4 to 1 billion hectares" Published online at OurWorldinData.org. https://ourworldindata.org/land-use-diets

12. #Why_Are_Chickens_Bigger_Today_Than_50_Years_Ago. Team, Enviroliteracy. "Why Are Chickens Bigger Today than 50 Years Ago?" The Environmental Literacy Council, 2 Mar. 2025, https://enviroliteracy.org/why-are-chickens-bigger-today-than-50-years-ago/

13. Medicine, Center for Veterinary. "Steroid Hormone Implants Used for Growth in Food-Producing Animals." U.S. Food and Drug Administration, FDA, 24 Oct. 2024, https://www.fda.gov/animal-veterinary/product-safety-information/steroid-hormone-implants-used-growth-food-producing-animals

14. Duke, Dick. "How Many Wild Animals Are Killed Each Year by Humans?" Geographic FAQ Hub: Answers to Your Global Questions, 21 June 2024, https://www.ncesc.com/geographic-faq/how-many-wild-animals-are-killed-each-year-by-humans/

www.ingramcontent.com/pod-product-compliance
Lightning Source LLC
LaVergne TN
LVHW021622080426
835510LV00019B/2717